STUPENDOUS AND TREMENDOUS TECHNOLOGY

TERRIFIC (AND TRAILBLAZING) TRANSPORTATION

ENTER A WORLD OF VISIONARY VEHICLES!

CLAUDIA MARTIN

Gareth Stevens PUBLISHING

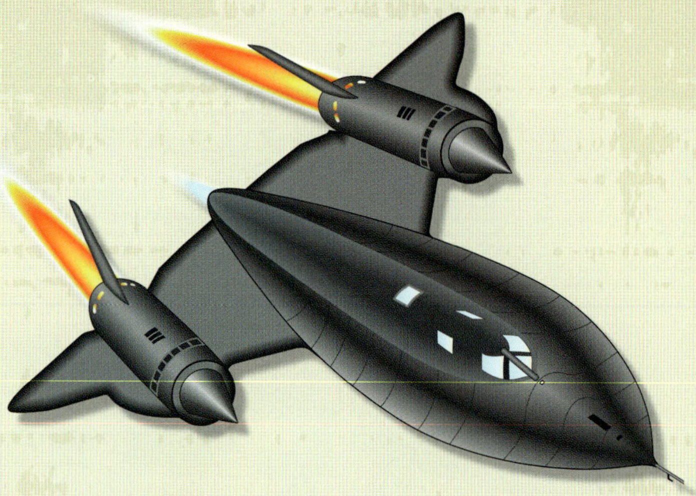

Please visit our website, www.garethstevens.com. For a free color catalog of all our high-quality books, call toll free 1-800-542-2595 or fax 1-877-542-2596.

Published in 2025 by
Gareth Stevens Publishing
2544 Clinton St.
Buffalo, NY 14224

First published in Great Britain in 2022 by Wayland

Author and editor:
Claudia Martin

Series designer:
Rocket Design (East Anglia) Ltd

Illustrator:
Steve Evans

Proofreader:
Annabel Savery

Cataloging-in-Publication Data

Names: Martin, Claudia.
Title: Terrific (and trailblazing) transportation / Claudia Martin.
Description: Buffalo, NY : Gareth Stevens Publishing, 2025. | Series: Stupendous and tremendous technology | Includes glossary and index.
Identifiers: ISBN 9781538294628 (pbk.) | ISBN 9781538294635 (library bound) | ISBN 9781538294642 (ebook)
Subjects: LCSH: Transportation engineering--Juvenile literature. | Transportation--Juvenile literature.
Classification: LCC TA1149.M37 2025 | DDC 629.04092--dc23

Illustrations by Steve Evans: front cover main, 1, 3tr, 3cr, 3br, 5b, 9b, 15br, 16cr, 16bl, 19b, 21b, 22cr, 23br, 25br, 27tr, 28br, 29cr, 29b, 31tr, 31cr.

Picture acknowledgements: iStock: legna69 4cl, duncan1890 6cl, ilbusca 6bl, anilyanik 9tl, kenmo 11bl, grimgram 21c; John T. Daniels: 23tl; NASA Langley Research Center: 25cl; order_242 from Chile: 11bc; Shutterstock: ikinugrihi front cover tr, Doremi front cover bg, Fouad A. Saad 2tr, 24c, 25tr, 30tl, Kamira 5cl, ONYXprj 5cr, HodagMedia 6cr, Nasky 7tl, 7tr, Dmitry Yashkin 7cr, Sudowoodo 7br, 31br, Sergey Merkulov 8c, 8b, Steve Cymro 10c, Westermak 10br, anton novik 11cl, BNP Design Studio 11cr, Sam Moores 11br, Everett Collection 12bl, CanadianPhotographer56 12br, Kit8.net 13c, NotionPic 13br, alenacepl 14cr, Pablo del Rio Sotelo 14b, Igogosha 15tr, cyo bo 17tl, Jiaye Liu 17tr, mTaira 17br, Rawpixel.com 18cl, Alvov 18c, Boyloso 18cr, WishnclickS 18bl, mooinblack 18bc, Dave Turner 18br, WindVector 19tr, Sergey Merkulov 20cr, Multipedia 22b, Valentine Illustrator 23cr, joshimerbin 26–27, 32, Vadim Sadovski/NASA 27bc; Sierra Nevada Space Systems: 27br.

All additional design elements from Shutterstock or drawn by designer.

Printed in the United States of America

CPSIA compliance information: Batch #CSGS25: For further information contact Gareth Stevens at 1-800-542-2595.

TERRIFIC AND TRAILBLAZING

CONTENTS

GETTING MOVING

Transportation is the movement of people or things from one place to another. Today, we can use speedy vehicles to travel over land and water and through air and space. But our transportation technology has taken thousands of years to develop ...

EVEN TODAY, DUGOUT CANOES ARE A USEFUL AND LOW-COST MODE OF TRANSPORTATION.

WHAT WAS THE EARLIEST VEHICLE?

The first vehicles were boats. The oldest discovered boat, called the Pesse canoe, is around 9,600 years old. It was found in the Netherlands, in northwestern Europe. It is a dugout canoe, made by hollowing out a tree trunk. Other early boats were rafts, woven from reeds. These plant materials were chosen because they float. Materials float if they are less dense than water. Density is a measure of how tightly packed the molecules are in a material.

WHAT ANIMALS WERE FIRST USED FOR TRANSPORT?

Around 5,500 years ago, humans had the idea that using animals to carry people and goods would be less tiring and quicker than walking. Ancestors of the donkey were probably the first animals used for transportation. Other animals used for early transportation, called pack animals, include camels and horses. Pack animals are still used for transportation in places where wheeled vehicles would not be practical, such as mountains and deserts.

WHERE WAS THE WHEEL INVENTED?

The wheel is thought to have been invented in Mesopotamia (an ancient region centered in modern Iraq). Wheels were being used on carts by around 5,500 years ago. Early wheels were solid wooden disks, often slices of tree trunks, with a hole in the center for a straight shaft called an axle. Wheels with spokes radiating from the center of the wheel did not appear for at least another thousand years. Spoked wheels are lighter than solid wheels.

SUPER SCIENCE

Before the invention of the wheel and axle, loads were often dragged over the ground on sleds – which was hard work! When a load is dragged, friction between the load and the ground slows down progress. Friction is a force between two surfaces that are sliding across each other. Friction works in the opposite direction to the one in which the object is trying to move. Compared with an object being dragged, there is little friction between the ground and the portion of the wheel's rim that touches it at any time.

BRILLIANT BIKES!

A bicycle is a two-wheeled, human-powered vehicle that requires the rider to balance carefully so they do not ... wobble ... and fall. The invention of the bicycle changed transportation forever, as it allows people to travel cheaply and (quite) quickly to wherever they want.

WHO INVENTED THE BICYCLE?

The modern bicycle was the work of several groundbreaking inventors:

KARL VON DRAIS

IN AROUND 1817, VON DRAIS INVENTED THE FIRST STEERABLE, TWO-WHEELED, HUMAN-POWERED MACHINE. UNFORTUNATELY, IT HAD NO PEDALS.

EUGÈNE MEYER

FROM 1869, THE PENNY-FARTHING'S HUGE FRONT WHEEL PROVIDED GREATER SPEED DUE TO ITS RIM TRAVELING A LARGER DISTANCE FOR EVERY ROTATION OF THE PEDALS BY THE RIDER'S LEGS.

JOHN KEMP STARLEY

IN 1885, STARLEY INVENTED THE SAFETY BICYCLE, WHICH WAS STEERED WITH THE FRONT WHEEL AND USED A CHAIN TO CARRY POWER FROM THE PEDALS TO THE BACK WHEEL. IT WAS MADE EXTREMELY POPULAR BY THE INVENTION OF AIR-FILLED TIRES BY JOHN BOYD DUNLOP IN 1888, MAKING THE RIDE LESS BUMPY.

HOW DO GEARS WORK?

Most modern bicycles have between three and thirty gears. Bicycle gears are tooth-edged wheels attached to the back wheel and linked to the pedals by a chain. When you use a higher gear, the chain is moved onto a smaller gear wheel. This makes the bicycle's back wheel turn more for every rotation of the pedals, giving high speed if you are on flat ground. Going into a lower gear moves the chain onto a bigger gear wheel. This is useful for going uphill, as each turn of the pedals covers a smaller distance but has more power.

HIGH GEAR

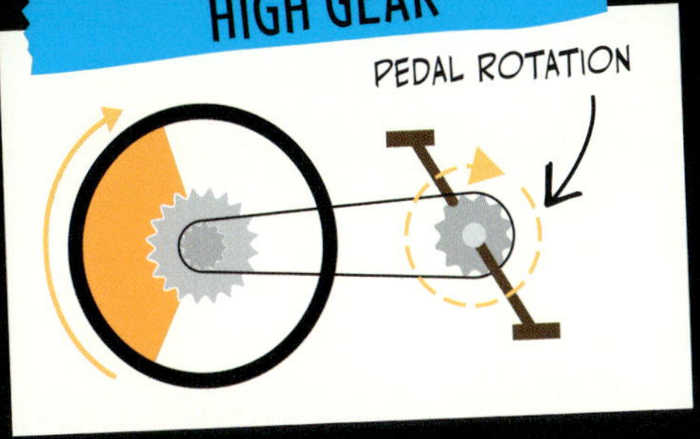

WHEN CYCLING UPHILL, USING A LOWER GEAR MEANS YOU HAVE TO PUT LESS FORCE INTO YOUR PEDALING.

LOW GEAR

HOW FAST CAN BIKES GO?

The fastest speed reached by a track bicycle on a cycling track is 200 meters (656 feet) in 9.1 seconds. Track bikes have taller wheels than many other bikes, which means the wheels travel farther for each rotation of the pedals. The handlebars are positioned lower than the saddle, making the rider bend forward, creating a smooth, aerodynamic shape. This means that they cut through the air easily.

Most bikes have spoked wheels, making them unlikely to be toppled over by a crosswind. Since track bicycles are used only indoors, many have aerodynamically shaped solid wheels, which allow air to flow past them more easily than over spoked wheels.

A TRACK CYCLIST'S HELMET HAS AN AERODYNAMIC SHAPE.

FREAKY FACT

In 2018, Scotland's Jenny Graham became the fastest person to cycle around the world alone. Her 18,000-mile (29,000 km) journey (plus four flights and a boat ride) took 124 days, 10 hours, and 50 minutes. Her bike had a strong steel frame that could withstand bouncing over tough terrain.

STEAMING AHEAD

The invention of a successful steam engine in 1712 led the way to the first vehicles that were powered neither by people nor by animals! A steam engine burns fuel to heat water, which produces steam ...

WHAT'S SO HOT ABOUT STEAM?

Steam can be used to turn wheels! Most 18th- and 19th-century steam engines heated water by burning coal.

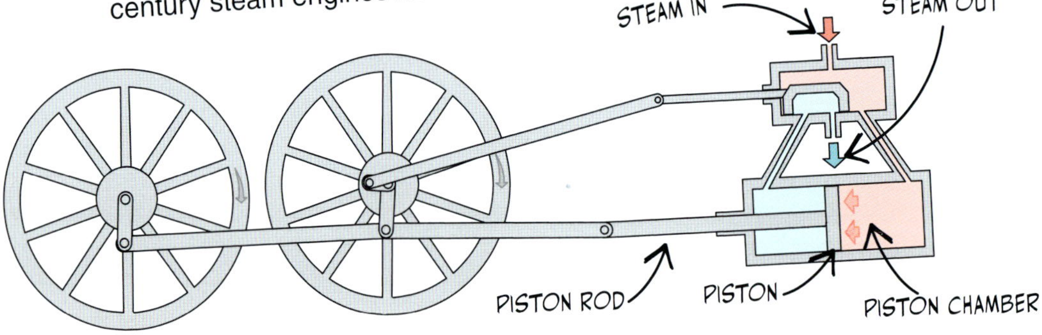

1 1. HOT STEAM SURGED INTO A PISTON CHAMBER, PUSHING THE PISTON TO THE LEFT. THE PISTON ROD GAVE THE WHEELS A HALF-TURN.

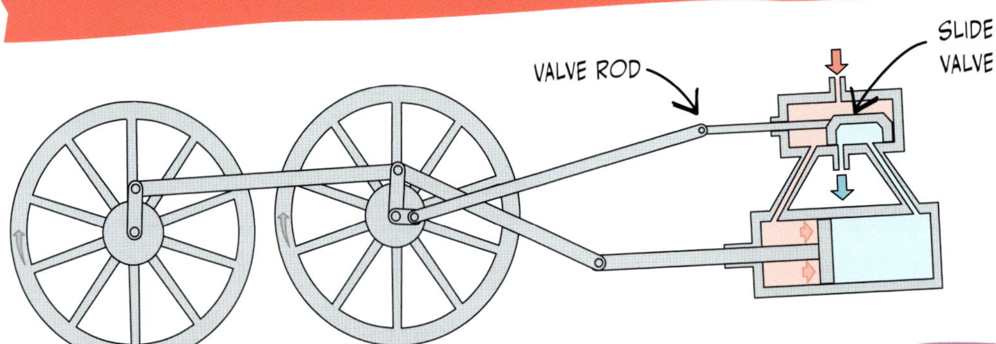

2 2. AS THE WHEELS TURNED, THE VALVE ROD PUSHED THE SLIDE VALVE TO THE RIGHT, WHICH SENT STEAM RUSHING INTO THE LEFT SIDE OF THE PISTON CHAMBER. THIS PUSHED THE PISTON TO THE RIGHT, GIVING THE WHEELS ANOTHER HALF-TURN. THIS PROCESS REPEATED OVER AND OVER, TURNING THE WHEELS ROUND AND ROUND.

WHEN WAS THE FIRST RAILWAY JOURNEY?

The first railway journey took place in 1804, powered by a steam locomotive designed by British engineer Richard Trevithick. A locomotive is a vehicle that provides the power for a train. Trevithick's locomotive traveled at around 2.4 mph (3.9 kph). The journey was along the tracks of the Penydarren Ironworks, in Wales. Until that journey, the tracks had been used by carts pulled by horses. The iron tracks had a raised edge that kept cart and locomotive wheels in place. By 1825, the first public passenger railway had been built, in northern England, followed by steam railways across the world.

WAS STEAM POWER JUST FOR TRAINS?

Steam engines were used not just to power trains, but for ships and buses too. The first truly successful steamboat was the *Charlotte Dundas*, built in Scotland in 1803. The engine powered a paddlewheel, a rotating frame with paddles that pushed water behind the boat, moving the boat forward. The first steam buses were running regular services by the 1830s. Some services continued into the 20th century, when they were abandoned in favor of vehicles powered by internal combustion engines (see page 10).

FREAKY FACT

In 1906, a steam-powered car called the *Stanley Rocket* broke the land speed record, the highest speed reached by a vehicle on land. American race car driver Fred Marriott reached 127.7 mph (205.5 kph).

COOL CARS

The car was a world-changing invention! It allows us to travel quickly to wherever we want, as long as it's on a road! Today, there are around 1.4 billion cars, but back in 1885 there were just one or two ...

WHO INVENTED THE CAR?

The first successful car was built by German inventor Karl Benz in 1885. Like most modern cars, his Benz Patent-Motorwagen was powered by an internal combustion engine, which burns liquid fuel, such as gasoline. Benz's engine had four strokes, or movements:

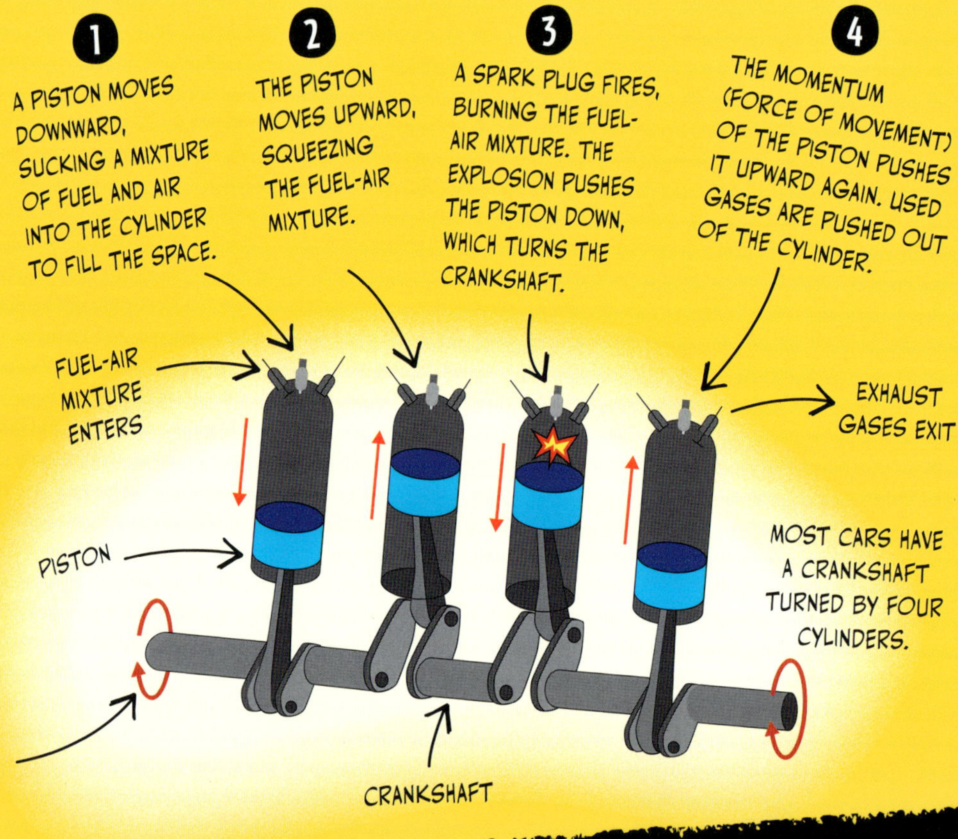

HOW FAST CAN A CAR DRIVE?

Today, the fastest commercially produced cars can reach over 280 mph (450 kph)! Unlike racing cars, commercially produced cars are built in factories and usually in large numbers. The top speed for a racing car – 763 mph (1,228 kph) – is held by ThrustSSC, which uses a jet engine (see page 24).

45 MPH (72 KPH)

1908: FORD'S MODEL T WAS THE FIRST CAR PRODUCED ON A FACTORY ASSEMBLY LINE, MAKING IT CHEAPER AND QUICKER TO PRODUCE.

HOW DOES AN AIRBAG WORK?

Most modern cars have airbags, which inflate if there is a collision, to protect passengers from the force of the impact. If a car hits something, it slows very rapidly. This sudden deceleration is detected by an accelerometer. This device measures how a small mass presses against its container. The accelerometer triggers heating elements in each airbag, which set off a small explosion. This releases nitrogen or argon gas, which flows into the nylon airbag at over 200 mph (300 kph).

SUPER SCIENCE

Seatbelts prevent a passenger's momentum from carrying them forward when the car stops suddenly. Today, cars use three-point seatbelts, which hold a passenger securely with a combined lap belt and diagonal belt across the chest. This design was invented in 1959 by car maker Volvo's Nils Bohlin. To save as many lives as possible, Volvo gave away the design for free.

WHEN THE DRIVER PUSHES AGAINST THE AIRBAG, THE BAG DEFLATES SO THE DRIVER IS NOT INJURED BY BOUNCING OFF IT. IT IS ESTIMATED THAT AIRBAGS HAVE SAVED MORE THAN 50,000 LIVES.

81 MPH (130 KPH)

1938: BUICK INTRODUCED A FLASHING TURN SIGNAL.

98 MPH (158 KPH)

1951: THE CHRYSLER IMPERIAL WAS THE FIRST COMMERCIALLY PRODUCED CAR TO HAVE POWER STEERING, WHICH USES A HYDRAULIC SYSTEM (USING SQUEEZED FLUID) TO MAKE IT EASIER TO TURN THE WHEELS.

283 MPH (455 KPH)

2020: THE AERODYNAMIC TUATARA HAS A TURBOCHARGED EIGHT-CYLINDER ENGINE. TURBOCHARGERS INCREASE AN INTERNAL COMBUSTION ENGINE'S POWER BY FORCING MORE AIR INTO THE CYLINDERS.

DRIVING INTO THE FUTURE

Much of today's top new tech for cars makes them safer to drive or better for the environment. With so many cars on the road, it's less important that they are extremely fast than that they are extremely responsible!

ARE ELECTRIC CARS A NEW IDEA?

Electric cars were invented in the late 19th century, but they were not popular during most of the 20th century. Concerns about climate change are making them more and more common today, with over 10 million sold so far. The problem with gasoline or diesel combustion engines is that they release carbon dioxide. This gas traps the sun's heat around Earth, which is raising the temperature of the air and oceans. One solution is electric cars, which are powered by motors that turn electricity into the movement of mechanical parts. The electric energy is stored in batteries, which can be plugged into a recharging point.

EARLY ELECTRIC

BY 1912, ELECTRIC CARS WERE VERY POPULAR, AS THEY WERE QUIET AND DID NOT RELEASE SMELLY FUMES. HOWEVER, THEY COULD DRIVE ONLY UP TO 40 MILES (65 KM) BEFORE RECHARGING. THEIR TOP SPEED WAS 20 MPH (32 KPH). AS INTERNAL COMBUSTION ENGINE CARS GOT FASTER AND SAFER, ELECTRIC CARS ALMOST FELL OUT OF USE.

TODAY'S ELECTRIC

MORE POWERFUL MOTORS ALLOW TODAY'S ELECTRIC RACING CARS TO REACH 341 MPH (549 KPH). THE TESLA MODEL 3 (PICTURED) CAN TRAVEL UP TO 348 MILES (560 KM) WITHOUT RECHARGING, THANKS TO THE DEVELOPMENT OF THE LITHIUM-ION BATTERY IN 1985. THESE RELEASE ELECTRICITY THROUGH A CHEMICAL REACTION, WHICH MOVES TINY ELECTRICALLY CHARGED PARTICLES – LITHIUM IONS – TO CREATE AN ELECTRIC CURRENT.

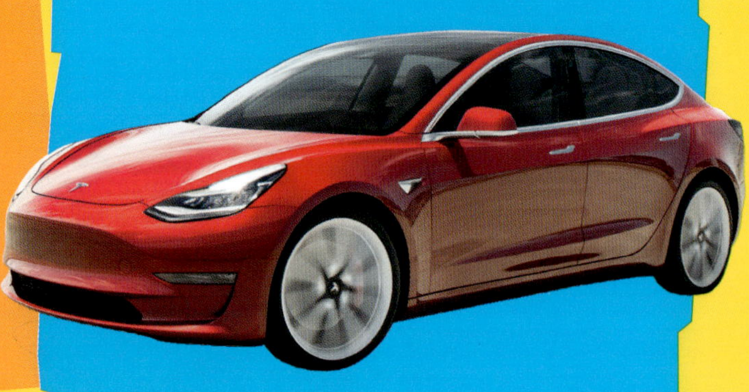

HOW DO CARS THINK FOR THEMSELVES?

Self-driving cars can "think" because they are controlled by a computer, which receives information from cameras and sensors, makes calculations, then adjusts speed and direction. A key sensor in most self-driving cars is lidar (light detection and ranging). Lidar sends out beams of light, which bounce off surrounding objects and back to a sensor. Since light travels at a constant speed, the time taken for the beam to return tells the computer the distance to another car or cyclist. Self-driving cars could make roads safer, since – if they are working perfectly – they do not make mistakes or break the speed limit.

FREAKY FACT

On average, a gasoline or diesel passenger car releases about 10,140 pounds (4,600 kg) of carbon dioxide per year. Since the invention of the internal combustion engine, the world's temperature has risen by 2°F (1°C).

HOW COULD SEAWATER FUEL CARS?

Seawater could be a source of hydrogen. Hydrogen is a fuel that can be burned in a car's combustion engine or used in a fuel cell to produce electricity. The only waste product of these processes is water. Pure hydrogen is not commonly found on Earth, but water is composed of hydrogen and oxygen and can be separated using electricity. Using seawater rather than freshwater would save the world's precious drinking water. This process still needs some work to ensure that the electricity used to produce the hydrogen is not more than the electricity produced from the hydrogen!

NO WHEELS!

Cars, buses, trucks, and motorcycles have wheels, but some amazing land vehicles do not. Wheels are ideal for rotating along roads, but as soon as a vehicle moves on to sand, mud, or snow, something a little bit different is needed.

WHY DON'T TANKS HAVE WHEELS?

Tanks are heavy vehicles used by the armed forces to travel across uneven, sandy, or wet ground. Tanks actually do have wheels, but they roll inside continuous tracks. Tracks spread the tank's weight so the wheels do not sink into soft ground or get caught on obstructions. A toothed wheel called a sprocket fits into grooves in the track and drives it along. A tank's track is made of tough steel plates. Many construction vehicles also use tracks, made of lighter and cheaper rubber strengthened by steel wires.

DURABLE DIGGER

TOUGH TANK

WHY DO SNOWMOBILES HAVE BOTH TRACKS AND SKIS?

The tracks at the rear of a snowmobile spread its weight on soft snow. The tracks are grooved to provide grip on the slippery surface. Tanks and diggers are slow-moving vehicles that do not need to turn quickly. Snowmobiles can reach 150 mph (240 kph), so they need better steering, provided by the skis. The direction of the skis is controlled by the handlebars, allowing the rider to steer in a similar way to a cyclist. The skis have upturned tips, which prevent them from getting wedged in deep snow.

SUPER SCIENCE

Amphibious vehicles are designed to travel both over land and water. In 2002, one amphibious vehicle, called *Snowbird 6*, used screws to achieve this! Its screw-shaped rotating cylinders carried it over the ice and through the water of the Arctic Ocean. On ice, the edges of the screws dug in, pulling the vehicle forward as they turned. In water, the turning of the screws pushed water behind the vehicle, moving the vehicle forward.

WHICH VEHICLES CAN WALK?

A dragline excavator is used in mining and large construction projects. The heaviest draglines weigh 14,000 tons (12, 700 mt) – more than 7,000 times the weight of an average car. A dragline has a long arm that dangles a bucket holding up to 5,900 cubic feet (168 cu m) of rock. Draglines are usually assembled on a construction site, but when they need to be moved from one part of a site to another, they walk! Neither wheels nor tracks could take the dragline's weight. The walking is done by immense "feet" that must be repositioned at each step. A dragline moves just a few yards per minute.

TERRIFIC TRAINS

There are many different types of train, from underground trains to trams that run on tracks on city streets. Most trains are powered by a diesel-burning internal combustion engine or by electricity.

WHAT WAS THE FIRST UNDERGROUND RAILWAY?

In 1863, the London Underground became the first underground railway. These are useful for cities, where the streets are already crowded. On the London Underground's first day, 38,000 passengers were carried on steam trains in tunnels beneath the city. From 1890, the system was switched to electricity, which is supplied to the trains' motors by an electrified rail. The trains have metal blocks called collector shoes. These make contact with the electrified rail that runs beside the track on which the trains' wheels turn.

HOW DO MAGNETS POWER TRAINS?

Maglev (short for "magnetic levitation") is a system for powering trains using two sets of very strong magnets. One set of magnets pushes the train about 5 inches (12 cm) above the track, to escape friction. Another set of magnets pushes and pulls the train forward. The system depends on the fact that magnets have two poles, north and south. The north pole of a magnet repels the north pole but attracts the south pole of another magnet. Maglev trains have been carrying passengers since 1984.

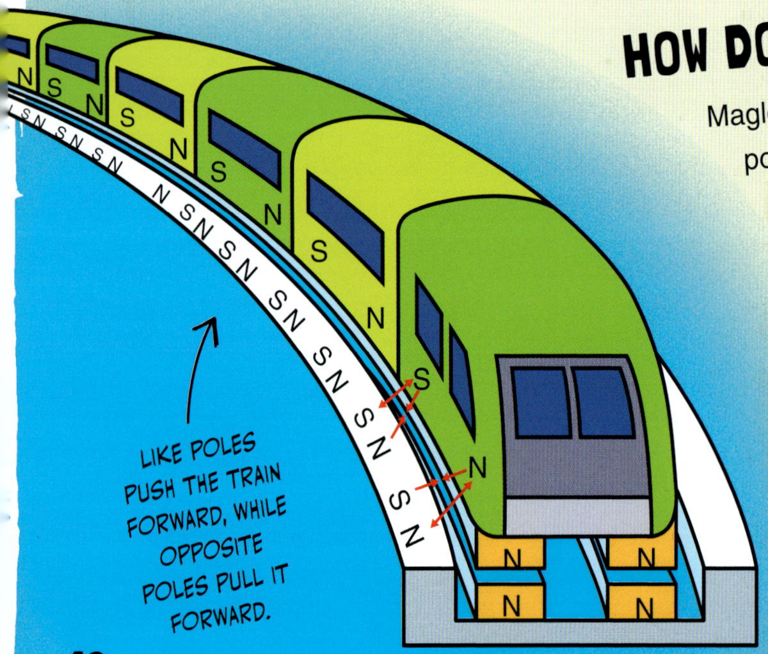

WHAT IS THE FASTEST TRAIN?

SHANGHAI MAGLEV

WITH A TOP SPEED OF 268 MPH (431 KPH), THIS IS THE FASTEST TRAIN IN THE WORLD. THE TRAIN STARTED CARRYING PASSENGERS BETWEEN CHINA'S SHANGHAI PUDONG AIRPORT AND THE CITY OF SHANGHAI IN 2002.

FUXING

CHINA'S FUXING LONG-DISTANCE TRAIN CAN REACH 260 MPH (420 KPH). IT IS POWERED BY ELECTRIC MOTORS SUPPLIED BY ELECTRICITY FROM AN OVERHEAD WIRE, COLLECTED VIA A DEVICE CALLED A PANTOGRAPH.

SHINKANSEN E5

WITH A TOP SPEED OF 199 MPH (320 KPH) JAPAN'S SHINKANSEN TRAINS SHARE THIRD PLACE WITH SIMILAR LONG-DISTANCE ELECTRIC TRAINS AROUND THE WORLD, INCLUDING FRANCE'S TGV.

FREAKY FACT

The United States has the world's longest railway network, with tracks extending for over 155,000 miles (250,000 km). Libya, the world's 16th biggest country, is the largest country not to have a railway line at all.

SAIL AWAY!

Most boats move along partly through and partly over water, but some rush over it and some (see pages 20–21) travel under it! For a boat to move forward, it usually has to make a backward pushing force – just like you kick backward to roll forward on a skateboard.

HOW ARE BOATS POWERED?

Boats use a range of methods for moving along:

PADDLES

PADDLES AND OARS ARE USED TO PULL WATER BACKWARD, SENDING THE BOAT THE OPPOSITE WAY.

SAILS

A SAIL FILLS WITH AIR, PUSHING THE BOAT ALONG WITH THE WIND.

POLE

IN SHALLOW WATER, A POLE CAN PUSH BACK AGAINST THE RIVERBED.

PROPELLERS

IN A MOTORBOAT, AN ENGINE TURNS PROPELLERS WITH ANGLED BLADES, SENDING WATER RUSHING BEHIND IT.

PUMP

JET SKIS USE ENGINES TO POWER PUMPS THAT SHOOT A JET OF WATER BEHIND THEM.

FANS

A HOVERCRAFT USES ENGINE-POWERED FANS TO TRAP A CUSHION OF AIR TO FLOAT OVER, AS WELL AS FANS THAT PUSH AIR BEHIND IT.

WHY DON'T SAILBOATS ALWAYS TRAVEL THE WAY THE WIND IS BLOWING?

If you are on a sailboat and do not want to travel in the direction the wind is blowing, the sails must be positioned at an angle to the wind. If you want to sail almost directly into the wind, a triangular sail called a lateen hung at the front of the boat can be angled so it throws air behind it – actually pushing the boat forward. However, the wind will still push you off-course, so you can also steer by angling the rudder, a flat piece of wood or metal attached to the back of the boat. As water hits the rudder, it shoots off at an angle, steering the boat in the direction you want to go.

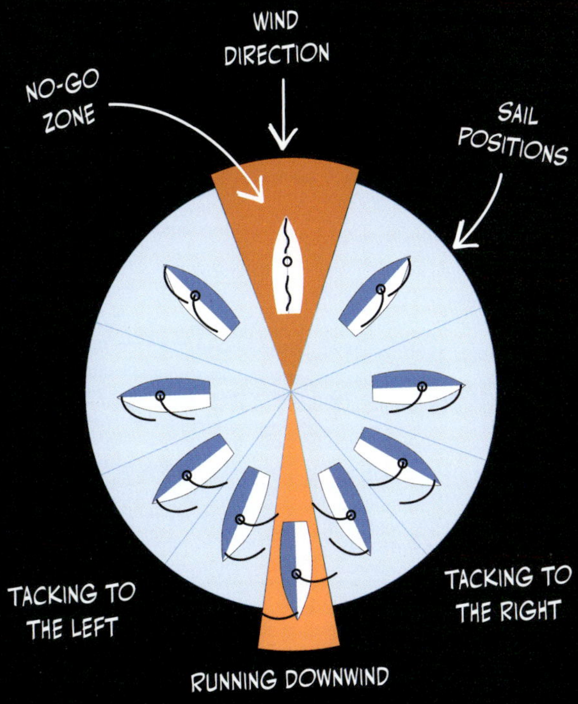

A SAILBOAT CAN SAIL IN ANY DIRECTION OTHER THAN DIRECTLY INTO THE WIND. INSTEAD, A SAILOR CAN ZIGZAG ALONG BY "TACKING" TO THE LEFT AND THEN TO THE RIGHT.

WHAT WAS THE BIGGEST SHIP IN THE WORLD?

The longest ship ever built was the tanker *Seawise Giant*, which carried oil across the oceans from 1979 to 2010. It was 1,504 feet (458 m) long and, when fully loaded, weighed 798,340 tons (724,240 mt). Since the ship was made of steel, which is far denser than water, why didn't it sink? Like other ships, *Seawise Giant* was not solid metal; it was largely filled with air. This made its average density less than the same volume of water.

SUPER SCIENCE

If a boat is rocked too far to one side by waves, it can capsize, tipping right over and possibly sinking. Some rescue lifeboats, which go out to sea in storms, are self-righting – which means they always return to being upright. The boat's wheelhouse, where the crew sits, is sealed shut, so it acts like an air-filled balloon that floats to the surface.

DIVING DEEP

Submarines are watercraft designed to travel underwater. They were originally built for the armed forces, but today submarines are also used by scientists for exploring the oceans. To travel to the deepest depths, scientists use small, light vehicles known as submersibles.

HOW DO SUBMARINES SINK AND FLOAT?

Submarines need to sink beneath the water surface – and come up again! To sink, valves are opened so that tanks, called ballast tanks, fill with water. This makes the submarine denser, so it sinks. A submarine has a supply of compressed air onboard. Oxygen can also be made from water using electricity (see page 13). When the submarine wants to surface, air is pumped into the tanks, forcing out the water. This makes the submarine less dense than the surrounding water, so it rises.

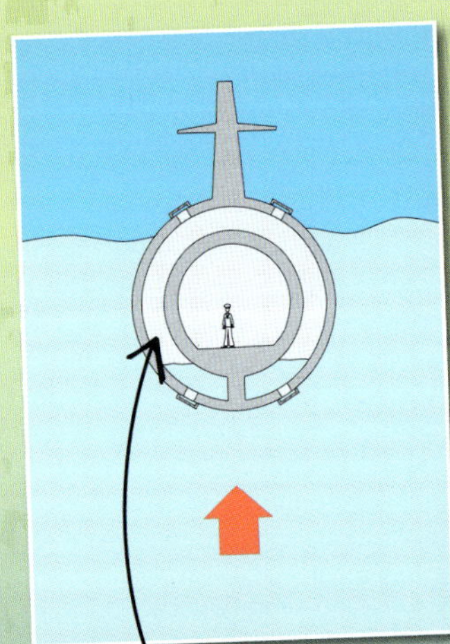
AT THE SURFACE, THE BALLAST TANKS CONTAIN AIR.

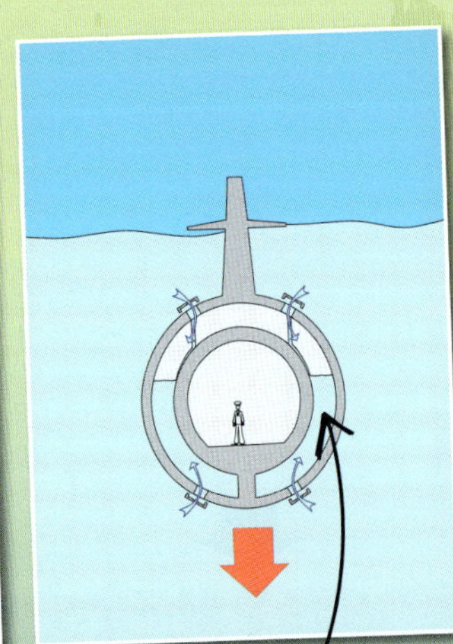
TO SINK, WATER IS ALLOWED TO FLOW INTO THE BALLAST TANKS.

HOW DEEP CAN WE DIVE?

The problem with deep diving is water pressure, or the weight of water. Without protection, the human body cannot survive pressure deeper than around 330 feet (100 m). To withstand the pressure, most submarines have two hulls, one inside the other. Even so, full-sized submarines cannot dive deeper than 985 feet (300 m). However, little submersibles have traveled to the ocean's deepest point, 36,037 feet (10,984 m) in the Mariana Trench, where the pressure is 1,071 times greater than at the surface. A submersible is largely round, a much stronger shape than the cylinder shape needed to house the crew on a big submarine. While a submarine's equipment would fail in the Mariana Trench, a submersible is supplied with power and air through tubes and wires from the surface or remains underwater for just a short time.

WHY DO SOME SUBMARINES USE NUCLEAR POWER?

Many military submarines use a nuclear reactor for power. This means they do not have to return to the surface frequently, unlike craft powered by internal combustion engines, which need air to function (see page 10). A nuclear reactor splits atoms of uranium to release heat. The heat creates steam that flows through wheels called turbines. These drive the submarine's propellers.

SUPER SCIENCE

Submarines navigate underwater using a system called sonar (sound navigation and ranging). Sound waves are useful underwater as they travel farther in water than other forms of energy, such as light. A sonar system sends out pulses of sound, then waits for their echo as they bounce back from other ships and the ocean floor.

UP IN THE AIR

There are two main ways of getting airborne. The first is in a vehicle, such as a hot-air balloon, that floats because it is lighter than air. The second – and much more difficult – method is in a vehicle that is heavier than air, such as an airplane or helicopter ...

WHO WAS THE FIRST HUMAN TO MAKE A PILOTED FLIGHT?

The first person to rise up into the air was Jacques-Étienne Montgolfier, in 1783, in a hot-air balloon he built with his brother. Hot-air balloons float because the air inside the balloon is heated by a burner, giving the air molecules more energy to dart around and spread out. Some of the air escapes from the balloon, making the air inside the balloon less dense (lighter) than the air outside the balloon. Everything on Earth is pulled by gravity, but a less dense object is pulled less strongly than a denser object. This means the cooler air outside the balloon is pulled more strongly downward, making it sink – and pushing the balloon up.

THE *WRIGHT FLYER* WAS PUSHED FORWARD BY THE TURNING OF ITS PROPELLERS, BUT IT WAS LIFT THAT KEPT IT IN THE AIR – FOR A MOMENT!

WHO WERE THE WRIGHT BROTHERS?

Orville and Wilbur Wright made the world's first successful heavier-than-air flight on their plane *Wright Flyer*, in 1903. Getting an airplane off the ground depends on a force called lift. An airplane's wings are shaped so that – as the plane flies forward – air moves faster over the top of the wing than below the wing. The faster-moving air exerts less pressure, so the greater air pressure beneath the wing pushes the plane upward.

WHY DIDN'T PAUL CORNU SPIN ROUND AND ROUND?

Paul Cornu made the first helicopter flight in 1907. A helicopter is lifted by the spinning of its main rotor. Like the wings of an aircraft, the rotor creates lift. The rotor creates such a downward rush of air that the helicopter is blown upward! In a modern helicopter, a tail rotor works against torque. Torque is a force created by rotating movement. If a helicopter had only its main rotor, torque would make the helicopter spin around in the opposite direction from the main rotor. The tail rotor turns vertically, creating a horizontal force that prevents the helicopter from spinning. Paul Cornu's helicopter did not have a tail rotor: it had two main rotors, spinning in opposite directions to balance each other.

FREAKY FACT

In 1928, the first regular moneymaking flights across the Atlantic Ocean were made not by airplane, but by an airship: the Graf Zeppelin. This was filled with hydrogen gas, which is much lighter than air.

CORNU LIFTED ABOUT 1 FOOT (30 CM) OFF THE GROUND.

POWERFUL PLANES

On average, more than 4 billion passengers board airplanes every year. These passenger planes can reach air speeds of over 620 mph (1,000 kph). Today's aircraft are powered by extraordinary jet or rocket engines – or perhaps even by sunlight.

HOW DOES A JET ENGINE WORK?

Most large passenger planes are powered by jet engines called turbofans. A jet engine creates thrust (a force that pushes a plane forward) by expelling a backward jet of gas.

1 THE FAN SUCKS IN AIR.

5 THE SUPER-HOT, SUPER-FAST GAS SHOOTS OUT BEHIND THE ENGINE.

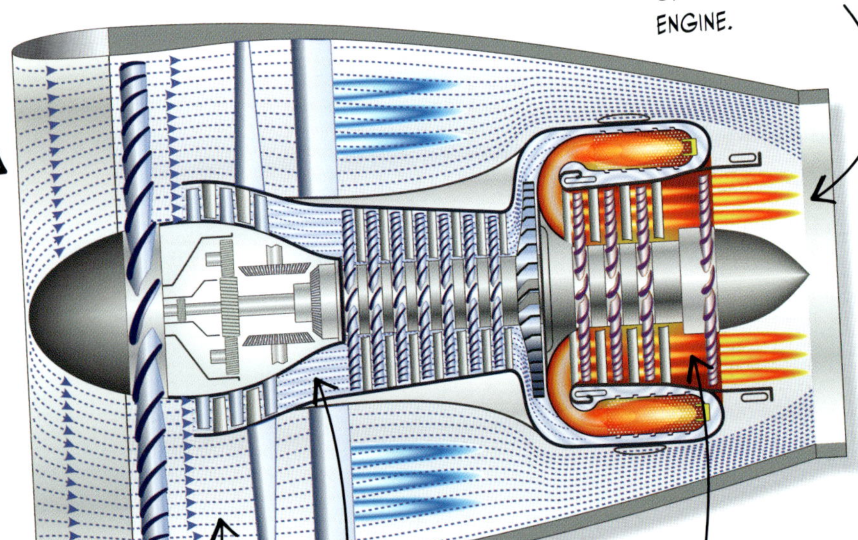

2 SOME AIR, CALLED BYPASS AIR, TRAVELS THROUGH DUCTS, COOLING THE ENGINE AND CREATING EXTRA THRUST.

3 SOME AIR ENTERS THE COMPRESSOR, WHERE IT IS SPED UP AND SQUEEZED BY A SERIES OF SPINNING BLADES.

4 THE COMPRESSOR AIR ENTERS THE COMBUSTOR, WHERE IT IS MIXED WITH LIQUID FUEL AND SET ALIGHT.

WHAT WAS THE FIRST AIRCRAFT TO FLY FASTER THAN SOUND?

Supersonic aircraft are those that fly faster than the speed of sound: 768 mph (1,236 kph), known as Mach 1. If an aircraft reaches Mach 2, it is traveling at twice the speed of sound. The first aircraft to reach Mach 1 in level flight was Bell X-1, in 1947.

LOCKHEED SR-71 "BLACKBIRD"

CURRENTLY THE WORLD'S FASTEST AIRCRAFT, "BLACKBIRD" IS POWERED BY TWO TURBOFAN ENGINES.

BELL X-1

BELL X-1 HAD ROCKET ENGINES, WHICH WORK IN A SIMILAR WAY TO JET ENGINES, BY EXPELLING HOT GAS, BUT DO NOT TAKE IN OXYGEN TO MIX WITH THEIR FUEL (WHICH MAKES THEM USEFUL IN SPACE, WHERE THERE IS NO OXYGEN).

FREAKY FACT

Weighing 628,317 pounds (285,000 kg), the world's heaviest plane is the An-225 Mriya. Its six turbofan engines and 290-foot (88 m) wide wings can generate enough thrust and lift to carry cargo weighing up to 782,641 pounds (355,000 kg).

WHICH PLANES DON'T NEED FUEL?

Solar planes do not need to burn fuel, which makes them much healthier for the environment than most planes. In 2016, *Solar Impulse 2* was the first solar plane to complete a round-the-world flight, although it had to stop several times along the way. The plane had solar panels along its 236-foot (71.9 m) wide wings. These turned sunlight into electricity to power its propellers. Although solar planes still need some work, they are a very exciting new technology ...

SPECTACULAR SPACECRAFT

Most crewed spacecraft are space capsules, which are lifted into space by rockets. After completing their mission, the crew lands in the ocean or desert in a wingless reentry capsule, their fall through the atmosphere slowed by a parachute.

WHAT IS THE MOST POWERFUL ROCKET?

The most powerful rocket ever used was the United States's Saturn V. It could lift 310,000 pounds (140,000 kg) into orbit around Earth. To overcome the pull of Earth's gravity, which can be done only by reaching a speed of 25,039 miles (40,320 km) per hour, rockets have to be large and carry lots of fuel. They are discarded after reaching space, leaving the light space capsule to continue alone. Saturn V had three stages, or parts, each of which in turn fired its rocket engines until it had used up its fuel and then separated, either falling into the ocean or staying in space.

FREAKY FACT

The vehicle that has traveled farthest is Voyager 1, an uncrewed space probe now 14.2 billion miles (22.8 billion km) from Earth. In comparison, the longest distance traveled by any single car is 3 million miles (4.8 million km).

HOW FAR HAVE CREWED SPACE CAPSULES TRAVELED FROM EARTH?

Apollo 13 was the space capsule that traveled farthest from Earth, as it flew around to the far side of the moon, 248,655 miles (400,171 km) from Earth, in 1970. The capsule had two connected parts: the cone-shaped command module, a cabin that housed the crew; and the cylinder-shaped service module, which housed the engine, electrical power, and food.

ON THE WAY HOME, JUST BEFORE REENTRY INTO EARTH'S ATMOSPHERE, THE TWO PARTS OF APOLLO 13 WERE DISCONNECTED. THE SERVICE MODULE BURNED UP FROM FRICTION WITH THE ATMOSPHERE.

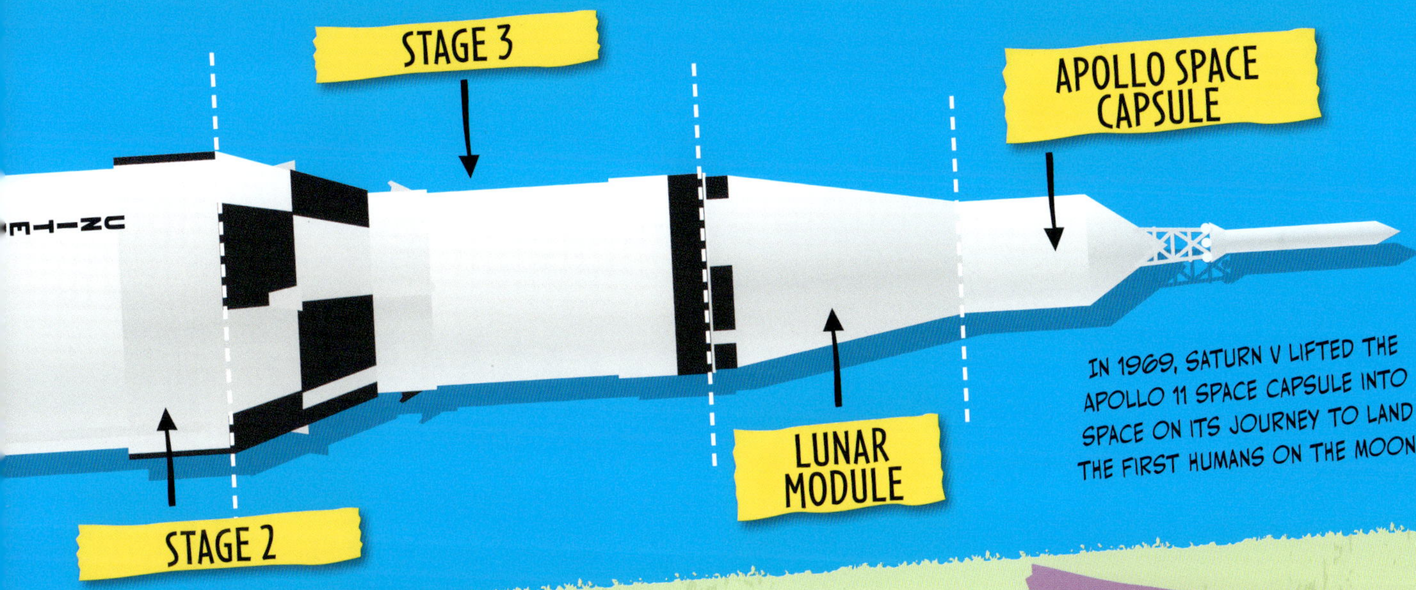

IN 1969, SATURN V LIFTED THE APOLLO 11 SPACE CAPSULE INTO SPACE ON ITS JOURNEY TO LAND THE FIRST HUMANS ON THE MOON.

WHAT'S USEFUL ABOUT SPACEPLANES?

Like space capsules, spaceplanes are launched into space by rockets that are dropped after doing their hard work. However, spaceplanes have wings so that they can fly back down to Earth's surface, rather than falling. Space capsules are not reusable, but spaceplanes are. However, spaceplanes have not yet flown higher than a low orbit around Earth.

THE FIVE SPACE SHUTTLES HAVE BEEN THE MOST SUCCESSFUL SPACEPLANES, FLYING 135 MISSIONS FROM 1981 TO 2011, INCLUDING JOURNEYS TO AND FROM THE INTERNATIONAL SPACE STATION.

SPACE SHUTTLE

DREAM CHASER

DUE TO LAUNCH SOON, DREAM CHASER WILL CARRY CARGO OR CREW TO THE INTERNATIONAL SPACE STATION.

ASTONISHING ACTIVITY:

DESIGN A VEHICLE

Now that you have read about some of the world's most terrific vehicles, try designing and advertising your own trailblazing car, bike, boat, train, plane ... or another type of vehicle entirely! Try this project with a team or just let your own imagination run wild.

YOU WILL NEED:

1. First of all, decide whether you would like your vehicle to travel on land, water, or air. It might even travel over more than one of these! If it travels over (or under) land, will it use roads or rails – or make its own way across rough ground?

2. Can you think of any problems you would like your vehicle to solve? Perhaps you are concerned about the pollution caused by internal combustion, jet, and rocket engines. Maybe you are worried about the high cost of many forms of transportation. Perhaps you would like to improve the availability of transportation for people who live in remote regions, deserts, or mountains. How might you solve these problems?

3. Whom or what will your vehicle carry?

4. Will your engine be powered by an engine or an electric motor? Will your energy source be gas, solar panels, hydrogen gas, or something else? Will your vehicle roll on wheels, fly with wings, walk on "feet," or be pushed along by sails?

5. Now it's time to produce an advertisement to sell your vehicle to a buyer. Think about how your buyer will use it. For example, is it for one person to travel to work or for lots of people to go on vacation in? Your ad should include a color drawing of your vehicle, as well as its name. It also needs a snappy phrase or a short paragraph to explain your vehicle. How can you convince your buyer or user that the vehicle is the perfect choice for them? What is unique or useful about it?

REVOLUTIONARY RESULT

When you are happy with your ad, show it to friends or family. Ask them if they would choose to buy or travel in your vehicle. Do they find your ideas trailblazing? Remember that some of the best ideas, like electric cars, were not a complete success at first. But that does not mean they are not the transportation of the future!

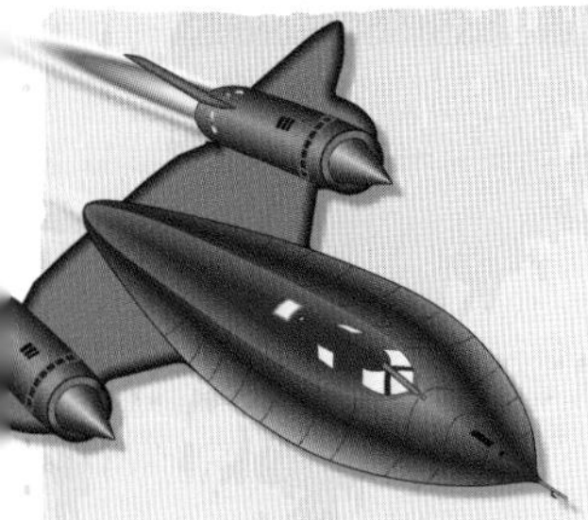

GLOSSARY

aerodynamic shaped to reduce the drag from air moving past

armed forces a country's army, navy, and air force

assembly line a series of machines and workers in a factory that build a product as it moves along the line

ballast heavy material placed in a ship or submarine to ensure it is stable

battery a container in which chemical energy is converted into electrical energy

carbon dioxide a gas that is naturally present in the atmosphere and is also released by burning coal, oil, and natural gas. An increase in carbon dioxide in the atmosphere is trapping the sun's heat and causing climate change

chemical reaction a process in which one or more substances are converted into different substances

climate change the warming of Earth's air and oceans, largely as a result of human activities, resulting in rising sea levels and an increase in extreme weather, such as wildfires and floods

coal a solid fuel made over millions of years from the remains of plants

combustion burning

compressed squeezed or pressed

crosswind a wind blowing across the direction of travel

deceleration slowing down

density a measure of how tightly packed the molecules are in a material

diesel a thick, heavy form of oil

electric motor a machine that changes electricity into movement

engine a machine that changes one or more forms of energy, such as fuel, into movement

engineer a person who designs and builds machines and structures

friction a force that resists the movement of two surfaces trying to slide across each other

fuel a material that can be burned to produce heat and power

fuel cell a device that uses hydrogen or other fuels to produce electricity

gasoline a light form of oil

gear a toothed wheel that changes the relationship between the speed of a driving mechanism, such as pedals or an engine, and the speed of the wheels

gravity a force that pulls all objects toward each other; the larger the object, the greater the pull of its gravity

hull the watertight body of a ship

hydrogen a gas that is barely present in the atmosphere but is present, in combination with oxygen, in water

internal combustion engine an engine that generates motion by burning gas or other fuels with air inside the engine

locomotive a powered railway vehicle used for pulling trains

momentum the force of an object in motion

oil a liquid fuel formed over millions of years from the remains of plants and animals

oxygen a gas that is naturally present in the atmosphere

piston a machine part that moves up and down, usually inside a cylinder or tube

pressure a pushing force

propeller a device, with two or more spinning blades, that makes a ship or aircraft move

rocket engine an engine that produces forward movement by burning fuel to make a backward jet of hot gases

rotation turning movement

sensor a device that detects physical properties, such as movement, heat, or light

steam the hot vapor produced when water is heated

tanker a vehicle that carries liquids

track a pair of long, fixed metal bars along which a train runs

FURTHER READING

BOOKS

Concept Cars (Motor Mania),
Rob Colson (Wayland, 2020)

The Big Countdown: Transport,
Ben Hubbard (Franklin Watts, 2020)

Trains, Planes and Ships (Awesome Engineering),
Sally Spray (Franklin Watts, 2017)

Transport (Building the World),
Paul Mason (Wayland, 2019)

Transport (Info Buzz),
Izzi Howell (Franklin Watts, 2021)

Working with Transport (Kid Engineer),
Sonya Newland (Wayland, 2020)

WEBSITES

Find out more about transportation on these websites:

www.ltmuseum.co.uk

https://thekidshouldseethis.com/post/an-animated-history-of-transportation-through-the-centuries

INDEX